John Winters

# Special Forces Top 10

First published by John Winters in 2017

Copyright © John Winters, 2017

This book was professionally typeset on Reedsy.
Find out more at reedsy.com

# Contents

# 1

# Introduction

Special Forces or Special Operations Forces are defined as military units that are stringently chosen and intensively trained to conduct special missions for a particular country's military, economic and political objectives.

With their flexible formation, these elite military units, in general, are led by the nation's highest commanding authorities and are equipped with powerful combat skills.

Special Forces units are usually shrouded in secrecy as they cannot be well-known to the general public – if the general public is even knowledgeable about their existence, that is. Their intimidating assignments typically extend beyond imagination, although their military accomplishments cannot be recognized. These highly elite soldiers are certainly considered heroes.

NATO Allied Joint Publication 3.5 defines Special Forces as "military activities implemented by specially equipped, trained, organized and designated forces, manned with chosen personnel, with the use of untraditional methods, techniques and tactics of deployment".

Such activities may be employed across the wide range of military operations, either on its own or with conventional forces to aid in the achievement of the preferred objective.

Politico-military factors may call for undercover or covert methods and the acceptance of military or political risk. Special Forces provide operational-level or strategic outcomes or are done where considerable political risk takes place.

It is important to note that Special Forces units are different from special-purpose infantry units like the British Navy's Royal Marine Commandos or the French Foreign Legion's 2nd Foreign Parachute Regiment.

This book contains comprehensive information on 10 of the best units in the world.

I want to dedicate this book to the brave men that serve in these units, and that make the world a better and safer place to live in.

I hope you enjoy this book!

# 2

# UNIT 10

### Danish Jaeger Corps
#### Brief History

The Danish Jaeger Corps is 230 years old, having been formed in 1785 and was then known as Jægercorpset i Sielland or The Hunter Corps of Zealand. The word Jaeger is Danish for "hunter." The modern version of the special force was founded on November 1, 1961, during the height of the Cold War (1992-95).

Denmark decided to create the Danish Jaeger Corps in response to the "Grey Period". Jaegers were tasked to gather intel as a long range reconnaissance patrol (LRRP) unit mainly because of their success in conducting parachute operations. Jaegers were deployed for the first time in 1995 when six of them were sent to Sarajevo, Bosnia. The Jaegers were part of the NATO peacekeeping force called the Stabilization Force or SFOR which is made up of military units from both NATO and non-NATO nations. The peacekeeping force was deployed after the Bosnian War to help keep the peace in the war-torn country. The Jaegercorps became a special operations force or SOF during the Cold War when they also had the task of performing long-range reconnaissance missions.

Becoming a Hunter is not for everyone. In fact, only 362 men have become bona fide members of the Danish Jaeger Corps. That figure only accounts for the period since it was remade in 1961 up to 2009. The current size of the corps is estimated to be around two hundred, though the number of Jaegers with operative status remains confidential. They are based in Aalborg Air Base.

Since its formation, the Hunter Corps has conducted numerous operations. As many as 308 Jaegers were deployed as part of the Kosovo Force or KFOR. The peacekeeping force which consisted of soldiers from 39 countries under the North Atlantic Treaty Organization (NATO) made its way to Kosovo in June 1999 to tackle threats and hostilities coming from the warring groups – the Federal Republic of Yugoslavia (FRY) and the Kosovo Liberation Army (KLA).

The Jaeger Corps, also referred to as The Elite, has participated in other special operations in Africa, the Balkans, and Iraq.

## Role and Duties

The Danish Jaeger Corps lives by the Latin slogan, Plus esse, quam simultatur which translates into Mere at være, end at synes and means "More to be, than to seem." Simply put, the members of the elite Hunter Corps have no need to be extensively known. They prefer to lurk in the shadows as they are more effective if anonymous.

A Jaeger or Hunter not only lives by the unit slogan, but he also has specific roles and duties to perform. Some of their primary tasks are Counter-Terrorism (CT), manhunting or acquiring High-Value Targets, and Special Reconnaissance (SR). They also conduct Arctic Warfare, Unconventional Warfare, Hostage Rescue, Combat Search and Rescue (CSAR), Covert Operations, and Mobility Operations. Other main responsibilities of the Jaeger Corps are Direct Action (DA), Quick Reaction Force (QRF), Protection Team (PT), and Parachute Deployment.

The Hunters are also adept in gathering intel and information, while also being actively involved in humanitarian missions.

### Recruitment and Selection

Like other special forces in the world, getting in the Danish Jaeger Corps is no easy task. To become a Jægersoldat, one needs to have the proper physical and mental well-being. It is not enough to just want to be in the corps; one needs to be capable of performing all the physical tasks required during training. For many, the most arduous part is the mental aspect of training to become a member of a prestigious group such as the Danish Jaeger Corps.

But before a prospective candidate can undergo training, he must go through the Basic Selection Test which lasts for two days. The applicants take written examinations on different subjects including English and Mathematics. They are also asked to write their autobiography.

After the written tests, the applicants undergo psychological evaluation.  A psychologist conducts interviews with the applicants to determine if they are emotionally and mentally capable of becoming a member of the elite force.

The applicants are then exposed to a series of tests to determine their physical abilities. The Cooper Test, in particular, is necessary to measure the physical condition of the applicant. This test, designed by Kenneth H. Cooper (a former Air Force Colonel who became a doctor of medicine and is now known as the Father of Aerobics) is done by simply having the patient or subject run as far as he could at a steady pace for twelve minutes. The purpose of the Cooper Test is to measure the condition of the subject, not how fast he can run.

The Core Muscle Strength and Stability Test or simply Core Test is also done to see how strong the subject's lower back and abdominal muscles are. The applicants also go through the Yo-yo test and other physical training exercises and tests.

To cap off the basic selection process, the applicants undergo medical examination to determine if they have no existing conditions that may prove detrimental to their ability to become a Jægersoldat.

Those who pass the Basic Selection Test proceed to the Pre-course. The applicant will first undergo the Pre-course, which is held six months before the Selection course. It is divided into three stages. Pre-course 1 takes up the first five days of training. During this time, the candidate is introduced to the different subjects involved in the course. They will also undergo tests to determine the fields they need to improve on which includes, among others, shooting skills, physical conditioning, orienteering, and swimming. One reason why the Pre-course is done months before the actual selection process is to give those who badly want to join the special forces some time to work on the things they need to work on.

The two-day Pre-course 2 involves further training and evaluation and is held four months prior to the Selection Course. During these two days, candidates undergo tougher tests and training. Another two days is needed for Pre-course 3 which happens two months before the Selection Course. It deals with more and even tougher training and more thorough evaluation. As a candidate goes through each Pre-course, the requirements become tougher. This is to cull out candidates who do not meet the standards of being a Jægersoldat.

The remaining candidates proceed to the 8-week Patrol Course. Here, the men are subjected to rigorous physical and mental tests. They go through each day learning different skills like orienteering, maritime insertion and extraction, cold water habituation, helicopter insertion and extraction, shooting, marching, survival, medic, demolition, and breaching. Their strength and endurance are also tested through different exercises including marching, running, hiking, and swimming. They are also given tests to measure their self-confidence which is necessary if you are to survive during missions.

After a week, the candidates who survive the Patrol Course proceed to The Selection Course. In eight more weeks, the candidates undergo a more difficult version of the previous course. At the end of this course, the candidates take a self-confidence test and those who pass are given the Jaegercorps insignia.

The Basic Parachuting and Combat Swimming Courses follow and those who complete these levels are accepted into training camp.

### Training

Once an applicant passes the selection process and all other courses, he is allowed to take part in training. The Basic SOF training lasts for 52 weeks. The men are subjected to eight fields particularly Arctic Warfare, CQB Shooting, High Altitude Low Opening Military Parachuting or HALO, Jungle Warfare, Mobility, Mountaineering, Weapons Specialist Training, and Specialist Training which tackles breaching and demolition, communications, intel gathering, medic, and sniper training. Each field is held in different parts in the world depending on what the training aims to achieve. Training for mountaineering, for example, is done in Switzerland where the mountains are treacherous and challenging at the least while Arctic Warfare training is held in Sweden especially during the winter season.

More demanding training follows the Basic Training. After a year, successful candidates are given the maroon beret which signifies they are now full-fledged members of the Hunter Corps. The maroon beret sports a brass emblem of a hunter's bugle. The Jaeger badge is also given to those who achieve operative status.

The hardship does not end when one becomes a Jaeger. To fight for country and survive in the process, Jaegers must be fit and stay on top of their game. Aside from their regular exercises and training, the Danish Jaeger Corps takes part in joint training exercises and operations. They usually do so with other Special Operations Forces under NATO and other coalition forces. Some of the Jaegers' regular training partners are the US Army Special Forces and US Navy SEALs, the Kommando Spezialkräfte of Germany, the Special Air Service Regiment or SASR of Australia, the New Zealand Special Air Service (NZ SAS), the Norwegian Forsvarets Spesialkommando (FSK), Sweden's Särskilda operationsgruppen, and the Danish Frogman Corps.

Joint training operations are usually held all over Europe where the forces involved improve on different skills required of Special Operations Forces including reconnaissance, parachute insertion techniques, hostage rescue training, medical training, Close Air Support training, and surviving different conditions particularly Arctic survival training.

### Prominent Operations

Former Hunter Thomas Rathsack released a book (Jaeger: At War with Denmark's Elite Special Forces,2015) detailing his many exploits as a member of the Jaeger Corps. His memoir allowed normal folks to get a glimpse of the dangerous operations that the corps participated in, specifically during the Global War on Terror.

One hundred members of the Hunter Corps were part of the Task Force K-Bar along with Special Forces from seven other countries. The operation lasted from October 2001 to April the following year. The objective of the 2,800-strong task force under the command of Captain Robert Harward of the US Navy SEALs was to conduct reconnaissance and surveillance missions in Afghanistan. The coalition was able to capture more than a hundred while putting an end to the lives of 115

Afghan terrorists. The Jaeger Corps received The Presidential Unit Citation for its part in the fight against Taliban and al-Qaeda forces.

In March 2002, members of the Jaeger Corps joined forces with ten other countries to fight the Taliban forces in Shah-I-Kot Valley and Arma Mountains in the province of Paktia, Afghanistan, as part of Operation Anaconda.

As part of the Afghan War, 700 Danish soldiers including members of the Hunter Corps were sent to the Taliban-controlled Helmand Province in Afghanistan under the British-led Operation Panther's Claw. The operation was a success after just a few months (June to July 2009). They were able to remove the terrorists from the area.

# 3

# UNIT 9

## Forsvarets Spesialkommando

### Brief History

The Forsvarets Spesialkommando or FSK is the Special Forces unit of Norway. The Norwegian Ministry of Defense created the elite group in 1982 in response to the increasing terrorist threats against the country and its interests, foremost of which are the oil platforms in the North Sea. However, the true origin of Norway's Armed Forces' Special Command goes back to the Second World War. During this gloomy period in history, a number of Norwegians served in the British Special Operations Executive while their country was under Nazi occupation. Some argue that these military personnel who belonged to Norwegian Independent Company 1 were the country's first Special Forces operatives.

The Fallskjermjegertroppen or the Parachute Ranger Platoon was formed in 1965, three years after the first Army Parachute Ranger School was established. This school later became known as the Army Ranger School or Hærens Jegerskole and would produce rangers trained in counter-terrorism. This group of specially-trained personnel would become the first members of the Forsvarets Spesialkommando.

Like most of the Special Forces around the world, the Forsvarets Spesialkommando is shrouded in mystery, especially since the Norwegian government hid the truth about the FSK. They denied the group existed, though the rumors persisted. Finally, a sort of admittance that the FSK exists was found in an article in Aftenposten, a local newspaper in the country. The article tells the story of a hijacking that took place in 1985 where members of the FSK were said to be on alert in case their services were needed. Though the FSK didn't need to leave their base at the village of Trandum to deal with the situation, the fact that it was acknowledged that the group exists was enough to cause a stir.

The FSK was mentioned by someone from the Norwegian Armed Forces who was talking about the hijacked SAS Flight 347 which happened on September 1993. However, it would take six more years before the FSK finally came out of the dark after Forsvarets Forum, the official magazine of the Norwegian Armed Forces, published an article about the Special Forces unit.

FSK has been awarded by the United States Armed Forces with the Presidential Unit Citation for its contributions in the War in Afghanistan. The current Chief of the FSK is St. Olav's Medal recipient Colonel Oberst Frode Kristoffersen who was appointed to the post in May 2014. He follows in the footsteps of Eirik Kristoffersen, his brother.

### Role and Duties

The Forsvarets Spesialkommando is Norway's primary weapon against terrorism and other threats. They are the men that the country depends on to perform counter-terrorism operations. These men have a take-no-prisoner approach to their missions as they are trained to kill perpetrators. The FSK not only aims to neutralize such threats, they are also involved in Special Reconnaissance (SR) missions, Combat Search and Rescue (CSAR), Direct Action (DA), Military Assistance (MA), and Collateral Activities (CA). Some specific roles they play are to gather intelligence, carry out military offensives, defend and protect personnel and departments, determine enemy supplies and their activities, and help in rescue missions of VIPs, among others.

Their services do not end with the end of warfare. The FSK also provides support to the Norwegian Police force and other law enforcement agencies when things get a little too out of hand like when people are taken hostage or a plane is hijacked anywhere in the country.

## Recruitment and Selection

Those who have served in the Norwegian Armed Forces care the only ones allowed to apply for the Forsvarets Spesialkommando. This is a good thing actually as the FSK can be assured that their recruits are already physically and mentally capable of going through the training. On the other side of the fence, applicants may feel that they have a good head start having had experience in military warfare and the physical and mental toughness to go through more training and specializations.

Don't be fooled by the promise, though, as being an operative of FSK is no walk in the park. The Selection process is proof that becoming an FSK is not for everyone, even experienced soldiers. In three days, applicants will go through numerous physical and mental tests to see who deserves to go to the next level which is another selection process. This time, however, the successful applicant will go through SOF selection. For three weeks, the candidate undergoes more difficult physical and mental exercises. What makes things even harder is that the men are given little food and allowed little sleep. Suffice to say, the number of recruits who fail or give up far outnumbers those who survive the process and allowed to go to training school.

## Training

Candidates who squeeze through the selection process move on to basic training which lasts about a year. They will go through each and every detail of being an SOF operative. Those who pass basic training become eligible for operational service in FSK where the recruits train in different specializations. A number of them prefer to become snipers though they can also choose to become a combat medic, a forward air controller, or other kinds of specialists.

## Prominent Operations

The most well-known operation where the FSK was deployed was the Kosovo War that lasted from February 1998 to June the following year. Norway took the side of Kosovo Albanian rebel group and fought with the Kosovo Liberation Army or KLA against the Yugoslav government forces. The Kosovo conflict ended when the Yugoslavs left Kosovo, thus allowing international presence.

The FSK was also involved in Operation Enduring Freedom where Norway's elite joined others to form the Coalition Special Operations. FSK was specifically sent to the South Afghanistan provinces of Helmand and Uruzgan as part of Task Force K-Bar. They also participated in Operation Anaconda along with the special operations forces of 10 other countries. Nowadays, FSK is involved in training new and current members of the Afghan National Police Crisis Response Unit in the city of Kabul, the capital of Afghanistan.

# 4

# UNIT 8

## USMC Force Recon

### Brief History

The United States Marine Corps Force Reconnaissance or simply USMC Force Recon owes its existence to the Amphibious Reconnaissance Battalion which had its heyday during the Second World War. Thanks to this team of Marines and Navy Corpsmen, other American ground forces were able to penetrate formerly uncharted territory that belonged to the enemy. The successful recon missions of the specialized battalion proved the importance of such operations and of Special Operations Forces.

Major James L. Jones commanded the Amphibious Reconnaissance Battalion after its inception. After the war had ended, the group was disbanded, and its members joined the infantry, Scout companies, or the division reconnaissance companies. The Amphib Recon Battalion was re-formed during the Korean War. In 1957, the company was re-branded as the 1st Force Reconnaissance Company under the guidance of Major Bruce F. Meyers.

Since then, Force Recon has played a valuable part in many a war or conflict in which the US became involved. These include the Vietnam War, the 1991 Persian Gulf War, and the Global War on Terrorism.

### Role and Duties

The USMC Force Recon's main duty is to perform deep reconnaissance or to gather intelligence while also engaging in small-scale offensive actions and short-duration strikes otherwise known as Direct Action (DA). Force Recon also provides direct support to the Marine Air-Ground Task Force.

One specific role of the FORECON is 'Green operations' or amphibious reconnaissance which includes beach and coastline recon, scout swimming, and small boat operations. The elite group is also responsible for maritime interdiction, countering piracy, and visit board search and seizure (VBSS).

### Recruitment and Selection

Before you go daydreaming of being a Force Recon operative, there are things you should know. Only citizens of the United Sates can join the elite group. Not only that, the applicant must take the Armed Services Vocational Aptitude Battery or ASVAB and have at least 105 on the GT score. The higher the score, the better are your chances to be accepted into the Marine Corps. Go through Marine Recruit Training and make sure not to give up.

Once the recruit finishes the course and becomes a certified Marine, he needs to serve for three to four years at the least. Once the Marine has indicated his interest in joining the Force Recon , he has to undergo the Physical Fitness test and achieve a score no lower than 285. The test involves running for three miles in 18 minutes, and completing 20 dead-hang pull-ups and 100 sit-ups in two minutes.

Other requirements before you can be admitted to Force Recon training are:
- -First class swimmer qualification

- -Complete Marine Rifleman Course
- -20/200 near visual acuity
- -Basic Reconnaissance Course (BRC)
- -Be a graduate of the Marine Special Operations School (MSOS)

## Training

The Mission Training Plan or MTP is the playbook of Force Recon training. The MTP has five stages or phases:

- **The first is Individual Training Phase .** Marines need to complete the Pre-deployment Training Program or PTP before they can go on to higher and harder phases. The PTP introduces the candidate to basic courses including Infantry Rifleman Course, Basic Reconnaissance Course, Survival, Evasion, Resistance and Escape (SERE), USMC Marine Corps Combatant Diver Course, Basic Airborne Course, Multi Mission Parachute Course, High Risk Personnel (HRP) Course, and, finally, Special Operations Training Group (SOTG).

It is common for Marines that complete the first phase to study and train further in special schools. These schools are simply other SOF units that can offer more knowledge and help further the skills of the Marines. Some of these special schools are Tactical Air Control Party, Scout Sniper Course, Pathfinder Course, Recon and Surveillance Leaders Course, Military Free Fall Jumpmaster School, HRST Master Course, and the U.S. Army Ranger School.

- **Phase two is Unit Training.**The Training Cell or T-Cell, which is handled by SNCOs (staff non-commissioned officers), involves three weeks of Advanced Long Range Communications Package, another three weeks for Weapons and Tactics Package, and the week-long Threat Weapons Familiarization Package. Other fields dealt with in this phase are Force Fires Package, Mobile Reconnaissance Package, Advanced Airborne Package, Combat Trauma Package, Amphibious Training Package, and Combatant Dive Package.

- **The Marine Expeditionary Unit [MEU(SOC)] Training**

This is the third phase,and lasts for six months. The SOTG or Special Operations Training Group handles this part of training. The Marines are further trained in direct action particularly in close quarters combat. They are also exposed to more advanced techniques regarding VBSS, gas/oil platform or GOPLAT, shipboard assaults, demolition, and cordon and search. Additionally, the Marines are trained further on humanitarian operations.

- **Phase 4 is otherwise known as MEU (SOC) Deployment.** This simply means the Marines are deployed for six months which the Force Recon calls Deployment Phases. The six months on board is filled with training exercises.

· **The last phase is the MEU (SOC) Post-Deployment Phase.** The Marines are allowed a military leave of thirty days after 18 months of training. This is the time the each member of the platoon must decide whether he will stay with the Force Recon, stay with MEU and recycle the loop, or to go back to his former assignment.

## Prominent Operations

USMC Force Recon companies were prominent figures during the Vietnam War. The 1st Force Reconnaissance Company performed recon to determine where the Americans can land, particularly along the beaches of Vietnam. The first platoon spearheaded by Captain David Whittingham was the first from the company to be deployed in Vietnam. The company, comprised of five platoons, was responsible for more than 2,200 recon missions.

After the 9/11 attacks, then–President George W. Bush countered with the Global War on Terrorism. FORECON was one of the many SOFs utilized to give the terrorists a dose of their own medicine.

# 5

# UNIT 7

## Shayetet 13

### Brief History

If the United States has the world-renowned US Navy SEALs, the Israeli Navy has the Shayetet 13 which translates into Flotilla 13. Israel's elite naval special force was formed in 1948 by Medal of Valor recipient and former commander of the Israeli Navy, the late Yohai Ben-Nun.

The first members of the Shayetet 13 belonged to the naval branch of the Haganah – the Palyam. The Haganah was a Yishuv (Jewish) underground military group formed in 1920 which evolved into the Zeva Haganah Le-Yisrael or Israel Defense Forces in 1948. The Haganah was instrumental in providing protection during the Arab riots of 1929. Within the ranks of the Haganah was the Palmach, the group's special fighting force to which the Palyam belongs.

The Palyam was the tenth company under Palmach's 4th Battalion and was responsible for underwater activity, including demolitions. The Palyam, however, was more known for escorting a number of ships and in the process helping around 70,000 Jewish immigrants reach safety. Out of the estimated 400 Palyamnik marines, Yohai Ben-Nun chose those with experience and expertise in maritime sabotage to form Shayetet 13.

Shayetet 13 is one of the three Special Operations Forces units of the Israel Defense Forces or IDF. The Shaldag Unit and the Sayeret Matkal are the other two. The S'13 is deemed as one of the best Special Operations Forces in the world and is commonly ranked at the same level as the US Navy SEALs and the Special Boat Service of Great Britain.

Little is known about S'13 as they prefer to keep details about their group to themselves, especially since most of their missions are highly classified, hence their nickname "the silent men". The group is so shrouded in secrecy that it was only in 1960 when Shayetet 13 made its presence known to the rest of the world and up until now they prefer that their operations and the identities of their operators remain secret.

Though the elite commando group prefers to stay mum about their missions especially before and as these happen, it cannot be helped if news leaks out after they successfully accomplish their operations. In early 2014, Shayetet 13 made news after a successful mission (Operation Full Disclosure) where they captured the KLOS-C, an Iranian weapons ship that was then traveling through international waters.

In its earlier years, the Shayetet 13 engaged in numerous operations to different results. The 1956 Suez Crisis, for example, saw the elite commando group failing in their reconnaissance missions. Another failed mission dubbed Operation Yovel occurred on July 9, 1958, when the Shayetet 13 attempted to infiltrate the Beirut harbor. Before they were able to complete the mission, the commandos were discovered and had to retreat after engaging the enemy in a gunfight. The Special Forces unit failed another mission in 1966 when they were unable to retrieve a downed MiG jet fighter of the Syrian Air Force. Their mission was to locate the plane, which crashed into the Sea of Galilee, and bring it to their side. After encountering numerically superior Syrian forces, the group had no choice but to retreat, allowing the Syrians to recover their downed aircraft.

But these failures are few compared to the many successful operations conducted by one of the best Special Forces in the world, some of which involved the seizure of armaments that were supposed to be delivered to Israel's enemies. The Shayetet 13 was able to intercept, board, and take over the ships carrying the weapons.

### Role and Duties
Each member of the Shayetet 13 is obligated to provide mandatory service for four and a half years whereas other units of the Israeli Special Forces only require their operators to serve the minimum three years.

In general, the Shayetet 13's main roles are to counter terrorism, gather maritime intelligence, and rescue maritime hostages. The special force also specializes in sabotage, sea to land incursions, and boarding.

The Shayetet 13 is composed of three specialized units. The Raids unit is in charge of land operations, particularly special recon, and direct action. However, the group also participates in sea operations where they conduct counter-terrorism and helps rescue victims of hostage situations. The second group is the Underwater Unit. They are responsible for underwater attacks and sabotage. They are also in charge of Beach Recon and Beachhead Recon and Security. The Above Water Unit's main task is to conduct sea surface attacks and provide transport units to and from the target area.

## Recruitment and Selection

The S'13 is the best of the best in the Israeli Navy and is even considered one of the best SOFs in the world. Suffice to say, becoming a member is no easy task. In fact, many see it as one of the most difficult courses in the Israel Defense Forces or IDF. It all begins with the selection process. Candidates who wish to join the elite force can join any of the two selection processes that take place each year. During the selection process, cadets undergo rigorous tests to determine their physical and mental condition. Due to the difficulty of the selection process wherein the cadets are not only physically battered but also subjected to stress and fear, medical personnel including psychologists are always on standby.

## Training

The survivors of the selection process then undergo basic and advanced infantry training for six months with the Nahal Infantry Brigade, the IDF's main infantry brigade. During the Preparation Phase held in their Atlit base, the recruits are trained in the use of advanced weapons and demolitions while also undergoing advanced infantry training and parachute training. This stage also tests the candidate's endurance by requiring each to go for extensive swims and marches. The cadets are taught how to operate watercrafts, as well. This phase lasts for three months.

Advanced Combat Diving is the next stage in training. Here, the cadets are exposed to the basics of combat diving where they should learn how to deal with cold and dark or cloudy water. The future S'13 member should know how to act in extreme underwater situations where his and his fellow soldiers' lives are at risk.

The final stage of training is the year-long Dedicated Phase. The recruits undergo a more demanding training where they are taught advanced diving techniques and how to parachute into the sea while also dealing with underwater demolitions and numerous sea-to-land expeditions. The recruits spend three weeks at the IDF School to focus on learning everything that needs to be learned on counter-terrorism. At the latter part of the final phase, the recruits are asked what specialization they are most interested in. There are three specialized groups or "professions" where the recruits are assigned to according to not only their interests but whether they excel in that field. These specializations or units, which were mentioned earlier, are diving or underwater, raids, and above water.

## Prominent Operations

The Shayetet 13 has been part of every war the country has been involved in, but one of the most prominent operations conducted by the elite force was during the Lebanon War of 1982. The First Lebanon War saw the IDF launching a military offensive against the Yasser Arafat-led Palestine Liberation Organization ,which was then operating in Southern Lebanon. The invasion was the direct result of an attempt on the life of Shlomo Argov, Israel's ambassador to the United Kingdom at the time, by men under Abu Nidal. While the military operation was successful, with the help of the Shayetet 13 and other Special Forces of the IDF, the Lebanon invasion resulted in the collapse of relations between Israel and the Maronites while also failing to establish peace between them and the Lebanese.

The Second Lebanon War happened in 2006 and saw the Israeli forces duke it out against their Hezbollah counterparts. The Shayetet 13 made its presence felt by seizing the MV Francop, which was carrying 500 tons of weapons and ammunitions belonging to Iran and was supposedly bound for Hezbollah. The elite commandos were also involved in the raid on the city of Tyre where around 30 Hezbollah leaders were killed.

The Palestinian War, which lasted from 2000 to 2005, was another war where the skills of the S'13 were put to good use. The commandos participated in a number of ground operations in Gaza, West Bank, and during the Battle for Jenin.

# 6

# UNIT 6

## Kommando Spezialkräfte

### Brief History

The Kommando Spezialkräfte (KSK) or Special Forces Command is Germany's top, most secretive, and most elite special operations military unit. The KSK is a vaunted and highly decorated group, having received awards and decorations from organizations such as the North Atlantic Treaty Organization (NATO), as well as from the USA and other countries. KSK operatives, handpicked from Germany's Bundeswehr army and trained under the Rapid Forces Division, are frequently deployed to strategic locations such as the Balkans and the Middle East, where they lead or participate in anti-terrorist operations.

It was not until long after the Cold War came to an end that Germany created a dedicated Special Forces unit. Before the Kommando Spezialkräfte was formed in 1996, counter-terrorist operations were delegated to and handled by different special military and police units. Between 1973 and 1996, the German government tasked the GSG 9, an elite police force that was formed as a response to the 1972 Munich Olympics hostage-taking, with all special operations and anti-terrorist activities. Before 1973, the Fernspäher (the army's Long-Distance Reconnaissance unit), the Kampfschwimmer (the navy's Combat Swimmers unit, also known as Frogmen), and the Sonderwaffenbegleitkompanien (the Special Weapon's Escort Companies) were the only German counterparts to the Special Forces units of other countries. Reconnaissance was handled by the Fernspäher, direct action by the Sonderwaffenbegleitkompanien, and maritime operations by the Kampfschwimmer. Since the Kommando Spezialkräfte was activated on April 1, 1997, most of the Fernspähkompanie were either assimilated into the KSK or disbanded.

### Roles and Duties

As with all military units in Germany, all deployments and activities of the Kommando Spezialkräfte have to be authorized by the Bundestag (the German Federal Assembly). The KSK has been involved in various low- and high-profile counter-terror operations in Europe and all over the world. The most well-known are those in Afghanistan, Bosnia and Herzegovina, and Kosovo. As with many Special Forces units of such status and caliber, most of the details of the KSK's special operations, such as casualty rates, are classified and kept secret even from the top-ranking officers of the Bundestag. This system has raised concerns, leading to a request for increased accountability and transparency in relation to future activities of the Kommando Spezialkräfte.

## Recruitment and Selection

Prior to 2005, only officers and non-commissioned officers of the German armed forces or Bundeswehr were eligible for service with the Kommando Spezialkräfte. Only they could apply and undergo the evaluation phase. Another pre-requisite was that applicants must have completed the Bundeswehr Commando Course or Einzelkämpfer-lehrgang. However, since 2005, applications have been open to civilians and junior enlisted personnel as long as they complete the Long Range Surveillance training, which lasts for 18 months, before undergoing the stringent Kommando Spezialkräfte selection process.

The KSK selection process consists of two phases. The first is a physical and psychological training circuit that lasts three weeks. This phase normally has a 40% pass rate. The second phase is a test of physical endurance that lasts three whole months. This phase normally has an 8-10% pass rate. The second phase is conducted in the Black Forest. During this time, applicants undergo a 90-hour cross-country run, a 100-kilometer march with heavy load, and an international Combat Survival Course lasting three weeks that is conducted at the international Special Operations Training Center (the former International Long Range Reconnaissance School) in Pfullendorf, Germany.

## Training

Once a candidate has successfully completed these phases, he is sent on to a two- or three-year training cycle of about 20 different courses at more than 17 different schools around the world. These courses involve training in deserts, jungles, mountains, Arctic environments, urban areas, underwater conditions, and counter-terrorism. Candidates go to Austria for training in mountain terrain, to Belize for jungle survival and combat, to Israel or El Paso, Texas for desert and bush experience, to Norway for training in Arctic conditions, and to San Diego, California for training at the US Naval Amphibious Base.

As of 2008, the Bundeswehr has aimed to increase the number of female applicants to the Kommando Spezialkräfte. This is, in part, an attempt to address the shortage of KSK personnel. Since its formation in 1996, the Kommando Spezialkräfte consisted only of male soldiers, but after the Bundeswehr opened all its units to female personnel in

2001, the KSK has also accepted female applicants.

## Prominent Operations

The Kommando Spezialkräfte was involved in the Global War on Terror in Afghanistan as early as 2002. This was the first time that German military personnel were in combat outside Europe after World War II. About a hundred KSK personnel were sent to Afghanistan in the early days of the war, along with a troop of about a thousand soldiers that constituted Germany's contribution to the International Security Assistance Force (ISAF).

In April 2014, KSK Special Forces units were deployed to the eastern Ukrainian city of Slavyansk to rescue the German Organization for Security and Cooperation in Europe (OSCE) inspectors who were kidnaped by pro-Russian separatists. The OSCE hostages consisted of four Germans, one Czech, one Polish, one Danish, and one Swedish national. The German-led OSCE team was detained after failing to disclose the true purpose of their visit to Slavyansk.

# 7

# UNIT 5

## The Green Berets

The Green Berets is an interesting and unique group of men who carry out some of the most important missions for the US government. They are formally called the US Army Special Forces. The Green Berets are trained a lot differently from most other soldiers in the US Army. They go through combat and special warfare training, but what makes them different is that they also undergo training in languages, culture, psychological warfare, diplomacy, politics and other unique skills.

## History

The Green Berets were founded during the World War II when they needed to perform missions that did not fall into any traditional military categories. In 1952, Brigadier General Robert McClure were granted permission by the US government to recruit and create a specialized unit to carry out highly classified and operations for the United States Army. In 1953, the first group of Special Forces Members was ready for deployment.

In 1961, President John F. Kennedy complimented the Green Berets for their professionalism, impressive skills, and bravery. When the president was assassinated, the Green Berets drew a black line on the brim of their berets to honor the fallen president. This black line became permanent in the Special Forces uniform.

The training center for new recruits was named after the President and is known as the John F. Kennedy Special Warfare Center. The Green Berets pay their respects to President Kennedy by putting a wreath on his grave every year.

### Joining the Green Berets

To join the Special Forces, one has to undergo a very robust, specialized and diverse training. The training takes a long time to complete so it could take a few years before being an official member of the Green Berets. Most men who join the Green Berets have university level education; some even have specialized post graduate degrees.

If you are a current soldier, the Green Berets allow volunteers to join the program if their rank is Private First Class or higher for the enlisted men. You have to be a Captain or higher if you are an officer. If you are a civilian who are not in the military, then you can also apply to join the Special Forces.

## The Q Course

The initial course for potential Special Forces members is called the Special Forces Qualification Course (SFQC) or simply the Q Course.The Special Forces Qualification Course (SFQC) starts with a 3-week preparation course to get recruits up to standard, this is followed by the Special Forces Assessment and Selection (SFAS).

The preparation course last for three weeks and focuses on a lot of physical and mental tests that tests the endurance of potential Green Berets. These Tests are designed to prepare them for an even more grueling training waiting for them at the Special Forces Assessment and Selection(SFAS). The tests include going through obstacle courses, marching and running for hours, calisthenics and land navigation. These training sometimes start during the early hours of the day when the volunteers have had very limited sleep and in the worst conditions possible.

After the 3-week preparation course, the training for SFAS will begin. Recruits will move on to SFAS if they completed the 3-week preparation course and passed. During the SFAS, the training includes some of the toughest training that a soldier can go through. These tasks are designed to test the physical, mental, and psychological capacity of a potential Green Beret. It is during this period that a lot of volunteers leave the course because they are not able to mentally or physically get through the training.

The SFAS tests the volunteers on how they work as a team. During the SFAS, you are divided into teams of 12. To succeed, you must work with your team to complete a series of tasks that are exhausting, grueling and arduous. The tests that volunteers are made to undergo include heavy lifting, swimming in extremely cold temperatures, rescue missions, land navigation, and getting out of mentally challenging situations. Many recruits get serious injuries during this training.

### Test of Mind and Body
Because the Green Berets take on missions that are extremely dangerous and unusual, the training that they undergo is designed to make them think independently and use a few items that are on hand to complete the objective. The training are modeled after real life scenarios like being held captive by the enemy or being tortured to give up valuable information.

The SFAS also include a series of psychological and logical tests like IQ tests, Defense Language Aptitude Battery test that the recruits also have to pass.The final test is an endurance test where the recruits are made to march 32 miles non-stop, and it includes real world simulations of scenarios that the potential Green Berets will potentially experience.

### Soldiers who do not qualify for the Q Course fall into the following categories:

- (1)Those who gave up without finishing the course or have voluntarily withdrawn are designated Not-to-Return(NTR). This means what it says, your career with the US Army Special Forces is over.
- (2)Soldiers who get injured are allowed to return to the course when they have recovered.
- (3)Recruits that successfully completed the course but are not selected are given the chance to retake the selection course again after 12 to 24 months.

When recruits have completed and passed the SFAS, they will then start training for the specific Areas of Operations(AOs) and will begin formal training in the Special Forces Qualifications Course (SFQC). The Areas of Operations selected could be the place you will be posted in the future.

### The following are the areas that the Special Forces operate in:

- (1)U.S. Northern Command – North America all the way up to the Arctic Circle and Northern Central America
- (2)U.S. European Command – This includes Western and Eastern Europe, North Asia, and Africa
- (3)U.S. Southern Command – This includes Central and South America and the Caribbean
- (4)U.S. Central Command – This includes the Middle East, Northeast Africa, and some areas of Eurasia

- (5)U.S. Pacific Command South – This includes Greenland, Asia, Indochina, all Pacific Islands and Australia

## The Q Course

Training in the Q Course include weapons and combat training, SERE (Survival, Evasion, Resistance, and Escape), land and sea navigation, survival, parachuting and scuba diving. Language and cultural training are also included.Independent thinking will be tested.

Foreign language classes will also ten to soldiers. You will also be trained in a particular specialty, and that could support cross training in other areas of training. This means that in case one member of the team is unable to perform his role, the other members of the team can replace him, and the team will still operate efficiently. Most Green Berets have at least two specialties that he as studied and have attained a level of mastery in them.

Because the Green Berets are a non-conventional unit, their training are tailored for all sorts of situations. Training like problem analysis and conflict resolution take up the most number of hours during the Q Course.

Unconventional weapons training and obtaining counterintelligence are also included. These days counter-terrorism training and obtaining intelligence on terrorists has also become a big part of the course.

After passing the Q Course, a graduation ceremony is given to the successful soldiers. This is where the soldiers get to wear their Green Beret for the first time.

## After the Q Course

Once you are fully trained, you will be grouped in a 12 man team. The team three the same team you passed the Q physical. Within the 12 man team, you will fill a specialized role that one other member of the team can fill in in case you are compromised. These teams are called the A-teams (Alpha Team).

There are two leaders within the A-team, and these are the Commanding Officer and a Warrant Officer, which is second in command. The rest of the team (10 members) will be assigned to five specialist positions so that each team will have two soldiers specializing in one position. This kind of unit structure makes it easier to divide the team into smaller groups of 6 members in case there is a situation that need them to split up.

**The five specialist positions and two leadership positions**
**that a Special Forces Operator can hold within the**
**A-team are the following:**
- Commanding Officer – the Commanding Officer is the highest ranked Special Forces member within the detachment unit. He

handles leading the group, explaining the nature of the mission to the team, and leading the team through the mission in the best way that he possibly can.

- Warrant Officer – A Warrant Officer, as mentioned earlier, is the second in command within the A-Team. HE is capable in taking over the command of the team in case the Commanding Officer is unable to lead the unit.

- Communications Sergeants– Communications Sergeants, are trained in handling highly sophisticated communications equipment. They are also well trained in broadcasting psychological broadcasts if needed. They handle transmitting intelligence gained from the enemy to the Special Operations Command (SOCOM). On operations, the Communications Sergeants carry the considerable extra weight of the communications equipment and handles the security of this high-value equipment.

- Intelligence and Operations Sergeants – They provide the team with information about the enemy before they go into battle. They are also responsible for identifying what sort of equipment the team will need in a particular situation and mission.

- Medical Officers – Medical Officers are trained medical doctors and a Qualified Special Forces Operator, this means they have two roles in the unit. Medical officers immersed in a particular operation can set up clinics and treat local patients while he is in the area. Medical Officers have to undergo 10 additional months of training after he has completed the Special Forces (Green Beret) training.

• Weapons Sergeants– Weapons Sergeants are experts in the use of a wide variety of weapons including the weapons used in the operational area they are stationed in. They can also provide weapons training to civilians if needed in operational areas.

• Engineer Sergeants– Engineer Sergeants are leaders when it comes to logistics in the unit. They are the navigators and pathfinders of the team. They lead the team through any terrain and can build bridges or other structures when needed.

Within the A-team, one group of 6 people is trained for airborne insertion that include jumping from very high altitudes. The other group of 6 is trained in various forms of underwater insertion. All 12 members of the A-team are trained in ground infiltration and exfiltration.

**The duties of the US Army Special Forces can be classified into three categories. These are wartime operations, post-hostility or peacetime missions, and humanitarian missions.**

Because Green Berets' mission is to blend into the operational areas they operate in, their humanitarian aid missions help them gain the trust and cooperation of the locals and to reach their objectives.

Special Forces operators also function as political advisers to political leaders and can support or lead non government organizations (NGOs) while stationed in their particular area of operation.

## Other Special Forces Courses

Some of the Green Beret graduates prefer to take up more specialized training after they complete the Q Course. These courses are more advanced skills training in areas of interest that will give them more flexibility as Special Forces operators. Let's take a look at some of the courses you can take after finishing the Q Course:

- -Combat Diver Qualification Course
- -Special Forces Master Mountaineer Course
- -Chemical Reconnaissance Detachment Training
- -Advanced Military Free Fall Parachutist Course
- -Special Forces Sniper Course

The path to becoming a Green Beret is long, arduous and psychologically demanding. You must be physically, mentally and emotionally strong to get your Green Beret. Sometimes even some of the best candidates fail. You must be ready for any possible scenario and be fully committed to anything that the training team throws at you. Are you up for the challenge?

# 8

# UNIT 4

SEAL TEAM SIX

The United States Naval Special Warfare Development Group or SEAL TEAM 6 as it is commonly known,is the US Navy's elite strike force.SEAL TEAM 6, the US Army's Delta Force, and the Air Force's 24th

Special Tactics Squadron form the Special Missions Group.This group is under the control of Joint Special Operations Command (JSOC).They have one goal.The goal is to identify and destroy terror cells worldwide.

To become a member of SEAL TEAM SIX is probably the pinnacle of any Navy SEAL's Career.Only the best of the best make it into SEAL TEAM SIX.All applicants come from within the SEAL TEAMS.That means you have to be a qualified SEAL Operator to apply for SEAL TEAM SIX.Being a SEAL is already a major achievement, but SEAL TEAM SIX is a step up.

So let's begin at the beginning and start at normal SEAL Training.
SEAL stands for Sea, Air and Land, which describes the elements in which the team operates.  Navy SEALs function in small units – usually composed of one to two men, although in some cases a platoon is composed of up to 16 personnel. The Navy SEALs are trained to do certain missions under any kind of situation and in any environment.

The US Navy SEALs' training takes place in urban areas, in the jungle, and in the dessert.

The operations of the Navy SEALs of the United States necessitate detailed planning as well as precise executions. The US Navy SEALs are trained to conduct assignments that fall into five major categories, which are as follows:

- Special Reconnaissance or SR – this includes initial surveys to obtaining data, manning observation locations as well as other kinds of surveillance (both covert and overt), where the objective is to obtain more information. This may involve following an enemy unit and reporting its location as well as obtaining hydrographic information (water and beach surveys) for landing.
- Counterterrorism or CT – this includes protecting troops and citizens, antiterrorist actions to prevent terrorist attacks, and direct action against terrorist attacks.
- Direct Action or DA – this involves moving against a specific enemy target. This may also involve ambushes, hostage rescues, or attacks on both water and land-based targets.
- Foreign International Defense or FID – training provided to foreign nationals with the aim of establishing relationships.
- Unconventional Warfare or UW – this involves the use of guerilla warfare strategies in battle. Guerilla warfare is described as small, mobile combat teams operating with the use of "unconventional" battle tactics such as demolitions, ambushing small enemy groups, creating diversions, destroying enemy supplies and other hit-and-run strategies.
- When the US Navy SEALs are not deployed, they undergo continuous training, both to develop their basic skills as well as to learn new techniques and skills that will make a difference once they are deployed.

## Navy SEALs training:

Training
The US Navy SEALs training is highly rigorous, having the reputation

as one of the best Special Forces around the world. There is over an 85% drop-out rate for US Navy SEALs training. An applicant for the US Navy SEALs spends more than a year in a number or formal training environments prior to being given the award of the Navy Enlisted Classification (NEC) and the Special Warfare Operator Naval Rating, or in the case of commissioned naval personnel, the designation of Naval Special Warfare Officer.

The following are the training pipeline in the US Navy SEALs:

- SEAL Qualification Training (SQT) for 26 weeks
- Parachute Jump School for three weeks
- Basic Underwater Demolition/SEAL (BUD/s) training for 24 weeks
- Naval Special Warfare Preparatory School for eight weeks
- Upon completion of the 26-week SQT, the trainees are awarded with the highly coveted Navy SEAL Trident and the designation of Navy SEALs. After which, they are assigned to a SEAL Delivery Vehicle (SDV) Team or SEAL Team and start a pre-deployment training for 18 months before they can be considered as deployable. The training is composed of the following:
- Squadron Integration Training (SIT) for six months
- Unit Level Training (ULT) for six months
- Professional Development – Individual Specialty Training (ProDev) for six months.

Enlisted SEALs who have a medical rating will initially attend the Advanced Medical Training Course for six months in Bragg, North Carolina prior to joining a group to become a SEAL medic. Enlisted SEALs pursuing officer posts will initially attend the Junior Officer Training Course to know more about the operations planning and how to conduct team briefings. It can take more than 2 and half years to train entirely a Navy SEAL for initial deployment.

## SEAL TEAM SIX TRAINING

Members that gets picked for SEAL TEAM SIX first go through an extensive interview process.The candidates that make it through the interview phase will go on to an eight-month Operators Training Course.The drop out rate for the training is extremely high.

The training a specialized type of training with similarities to DELTA Force. The training is very dangerous, and there has even been a loss of life in training.

The training is even more specialized training.The bulk of SEAL TEAM SIX Training is classified but what is known is that it includes the following: advanced climbing, advanced diving, advanced parachuting, self-defense, escape and evasion and interrogation resistance.The instructors for the training is civilian or military instructors.Training with the CIA and FBI is also part of training.

The following are some of the current and recent
operations of the US Navy Seals:

- 2001–Present The Navy SEALs have scoured the entire globe in
  search of war criminals, pirates and terrorists, conducting hostage
  rescue operations and incarcerating and killing high–ranking
  terrorist authorities. These operations were capped off in May
  2011 with the demise of the mastermind behind the September
  11 attacks, Osama bin Laden, in a highly exposed incursion in
  Pakistan.

2011 The Navy SEALs had a great hand in beating the Taliban group in
Afghanistan (Operation Anaconda) and forcing the senior leaders, as
well as Osama bin Laden, of al-Qaeda into hiding.

# 9

# UNIT 3

## The Special Boat Service

The Special Boat Service or SBS is an Elite Special Operations Warfare Unit of the United Kingdom Royal Navy. The SBS forms a very important part of the United Kingdom Special Forces (UKSF) along with an aviation wing, Special Forces Signals Regiment, the Special

Forces Support Group, the Special Reconnaissance Regiment and the Special Air Service (SAS).

The Special Boat Service is probably the one unit in this book that will be unknown to many.This is the way the SBS prefers it.They thrive in operating in the shadows and executing their missions with extreme precision.

All members of SBS are trained as combat divers, parachutists, boat handlers and are taught how to use mini submarines. The SBS can operate in the same role and capacity as the SAS, but their specialization is amphibious warfare. The SBS keeps a very close operational and training links with the US Navy's SEAL Team 6.

### Brief History
It was in July 1940 during the 2nd World War when the SBS was established as the Special Boat Section.After the Second World War, the SBS operated as a unit within the Royal Marines.In 1977, they were officially incorporated as a unit in the United Kingdom Special Forces.In 1987, their name was changed from the Special Boat Squadron to the Special Boat Service.

The SBS often gets confused by outsiders as the SAS, so many of their mission successes gets credited to the SAS.Their relative anonymity gives them great freedom and power to operate under the radar.Outside military circles, they are an unknown force.The SBS is an independent, multiskilled, amphibious Special Force.

There has long been a rivalry between the SBS and SAS. Historically this rivalry comes from the 2 Elite Regiments in the British armed forces, the Royal Navy's Elite Royal Marines Commandos, and the British Army's Elite Parachute Regiment. Historically the Royal Marines provide almost all the members to the SBS and Parachute Regiment most of the members to the SAS.

## Current Organizational Structure

The British Ministry of Defence provides no official information regarding the UK Special Forces; hence, there is little confirmable information available to the public. The SBS is in the operational command of the Director of Special Forces. The SBS is probably the most secretive Special Forces Unit in the world. Most of their training is classified.

**Headquarters:** The SBS Headquarters is in Poole, Dorset.

In 2002, the SBS was modernized and reformed along the lines of SAS, composed of 16 man troops instead of the conventional squadrons. Around 180 - 250 operators(operators is the term for special forces soldiers) compose the SBS. Upon qualification, SBS personnel are referred to as "Swimmer Canoeists.

These men are specialists in reconnaissance, demolition, self-defense, navigation, parachuting, submarine exits and entry, diving, and swimming.SBS operators are legendary for their mental toughness and guile.

## The SBS is composed of 4 active regiments and a single reserve troop:

- **S Squadron** – This squad is composed of experts in mini-submarines.The mini-subs is dispatched from large Royal Navy submarines and gives the SBS the capability to infiltrate enemy areas a long way from shore.The exit and entry of submarines are known to be highly dangerous work.The training has even caused some operators to lose their lives.
- **C Squadron**–These men are experts in operating 2-men Klepper canoes, and inflatable boats for insertion and extraction.This squadron's main focus is reconnaissance, surveillance and disruption of enemy activities behind enemy lines.
- **M squadron**– this group works against maritime terrorism and conducts ship boarding missions.These men also secure the UK oil rigs worldwide and is a major force in the fight against pirates around the globe.
- **SBS(R) or SBS Reserve troop**– this group supply individual reservists to work with the usual SBS team, rather than form independent groups.  Only personnel with experience in the military will be qualified for enlistment.Most Reservists are ex-Royal Marines.
- **X Squadron** – it was suggested that a new SBS group has been created from volunteers from both the SBS and SAS. This is a

special group of operators that are used for a wide variety of operations around the globe.

## SBS Process for Training, Selection, and Recruitment

The SBS in the previous years was manned completely by the Royal Marines. SBS volunteers are now recruited from all the British Armed Forces; however, the majority of SBS volunteers are still from the British Royal Marines Commandos.

Applicants who wish to work with SBS should have completed at least two years of standard service and will only be qualified to serve with the SBS following the completion of the tedious process of selection.

Before, the SBS has its own autonomous selection process. The selection process, however, has been incorporated into UKSF selection in 2002(along with choosing applicants for the SAS). All personnel of the UK Armed Forces may be considered for selection under the Special Forces ,although in history, the bulk of applicants comes from the Royal Navy's Royal Marines Commandos and the Army's Elite Parachute Regiment. In each year, there are two selection schedules – one in summer and another in winter. The teachers are regular personnel of the Special Air Service and Special Boat Service(SAS).

The selection starts with its first phase in Sennybridge, Wales, located at the Brecon Beacons and usually begins with around 200 applicants.The dropout rate is over 90%, This part of the selection process usually lasts for five weeks. Upon arrival, the applicants must have to satisfy two sets of tests – the Infantry Combat Fitness Test (CFT) and the Basic Fitness Test (BFT). After these two initial tests, the recruits move on to the hill phase.The applicants will have to complete a series of brutal country marches with the distances covered rising daily. After the last march at the end of the hill stage, the applicants should swim 2 miles in 90 minutes and run 4 miles in 30 minutes.Very few people pass the initial hill phase.The phase is legendary and is known to be brutal.The mental strength of applicants gets tested to their limits.

Applicants who have successfully completed the hill phase will move on to the jungle phase that is conducted in Malaysia, Brunei or Belize. In this phase, the applicants are taught how to survive in a jungle, moving in patrol formation and navigation.

Applicants who have successfully surpassed the jungle phase will go back to Hereford for further training in foreign weapons, battle plans and participate in combat survival exercises. The last and final exam is an escape and evasion test. The remaining applicants shall be formed into patrol and carry nothing aside from a tin can packed with survival tools. They are dressed in old 2nd World War uniforms and instructed to navigate to a certain point while they are hunted down by an infantry regiment. This test usually lasts for about a week and is followed by the last selection test called the Resistance To Interrogation (RTI). The RTI lasts for approximately 30-36 hours.

Upon successfully completing the RIT the remaining SBS applicants are moved to the Specialization Training with the Special Boat Service Training Wing.

Not much is known about SBS specialization training.What is known is that it's brutal.One part of their training is to row for 5 miles at night in deep sea in a two-man team until they reach land.Once they reach land, they should march for 30 miles.

Another part of training includes swimming for 2 miles and immediately swim two lengths of a pool and then getting out and jumping off a diving board.All of this happen while blindfolded and wearing full equipment.(The Telegraph,16 Sep 2002)

Members of the SBS wear a green commando beret, with their own cap badge.SBS Operators are highly skilled independent soldiers and are highly adaptable.SBS operators often work with agencies like MI5 or MI6, the British Intelligence Agencies.

SBS Operators don't often wear uniforms; they grow their hair longer than normal personal and often wear beards. They blend into society.

## The following are some of the current and recent operations of the SBS:

- 2012 Nigerian Hostage Rescue Attempt

A combined Nigerian-SBS force tried to rescue two Western hostages from radical Islamic kidnappers in Sokoto City, Nigeria. Unfortunately, the two hostages, an Italian and British citizen, were killed by their kidnappers during the assault.

- 2012 Safeguarding the Olympic Games

SBS troops were deployed in July-August 2012 to safeguard the Olympic sailing events on the south coast of England.

- 2011 SBS Carry out Surveillance Operations in Somalia

As part of its counter-piracy efforts, SBS troops implemented covert missions along the Somali coast

- 2011 SBS Troops Evacuate British Laborers from Libya

For two consecutive days, the SBS troops and RAF Special Forces evacuated western oil workers from numerous remote desert facilities.

- 2009 SBS Rescue Operations Failed

A rescue mission for two Britons captured by pirates fails when the SBS troops arrive too late.

- 2009 SBS Troops rescue a Journalist

The SBS has rescued a Journalist in Kunduz, Afghanistan from Taliban captors.

- 2004 Athens Olympics

SBS members trained and advised Greek naval special units in maritime counter-terrorism strategies, with a focus on safeguarding Athens' sea ports. It is also claimed that SBS provided advice and assistance in safeguarding the Queen Mary 2 cruise liner, as well as other ships that were docked in the port for the Olympic games.

- 2003 Iraq

The SBS troops were at the front line of the Iraq invasions. SBS members teamed up with the US Navy SEALs to safeguard the beaches of the Al Faw Peninsula. This has paved the way for the coalition of ground units. The SBS troops also played a major role in safeguarding the southern oil fields, which has kept Saddam from igniting the wells as he did in 1991 in Kuwait.

A roving SBS landrover patrol engaged in one of the most brutal Special Forces activities of the war when they were double-crossed by their guides/interpreters that led into an ambush. In the following engagement, the SBS team fired thousands of rounds at their enemies.

The war was so extreme that the SBS troops had no choice but to abandon some of their equipment, such as quad bikes and a Landrover. There have been conflicting accounts of the incident that circulated in the press.

In the southern city of Basra, SBS commandos were also active. One known movement was o call in the US airstrikes in an attempt to kill high-level Iraqi authorities such as Chemical Ali. It is also claimed that SBS has teamed up with MI6 operatives to destabilize and disrupt the Baathist regime in Basra, which has led to the successful capture by the British forces.

• 2002 – Present The Engagements in the Carribean

The SBS troops have been actively involved in some counter-narcotic activities in the Caribbean. The SBS teamed up with international and local law enforcers and is known to have carried out both interception and intelligence-gathering missions.

• 2001 Raid on the MV Nisha

UK intelligence services got a tip that the MV Nisha, which is a Mauritian cargo ship, was going to the London Port in November 2001 and was carrying terrorist items. Before MV Nisha can even reach the UK, a Royal Navy Regiment has intercepted it. The SBS troops were launched to board and secure the ship.

# 10

# UNIT 2

**THE DELTA FORCE**

The Delta Force is also commonly known as the 1st Special Forces Operational Detachment-Delta. Delta is under the control of the Joint Special Operations Command. The Delta Force is administratively supported by the United States Army Special Operations Command (USASOC); however, it is placed under the Joint Special Operations Command's operational control.

Delta Force and its counterpart in the Navy – SEAL TEAM SIX (Naval Special Warfare Development Group) – are the American Military's primary counter-terrorism forces.

Delta Force has one main objective, to deal with any and all serious threats against the Security of the United States and its allies. Delta Force has the capability to deal with any imaginable situation.They focus on unconventional warfare.They are modeled on the British Special Air Service(SAS) and operate in a similar fashion.Small groups of highly trained men that can conduct missions around the globe at a moment's notice.

The CIA (Central Intelligence Agency) recruits from the Delta Force and has a close relationship with Delta and often conduct operations jointly.Delta Force operators are a unit that operate in the shadows; officially they do not exist.

### Selection and Recruitment
Delta's main group of applicants are from the Special Forces(Green Berets) and the 75th Ranger Regiment.Members must be male and

have at least two years of military service.

Not much is known about Delta Force selection, but like I mentioned before they are modeled on the British SAS and so are their selection process.What is known about Delta selection is that their selection is a brutal SAS style breakdown that test every man to their absolute limits.Like the SAS, the initial selection tests are a series of marches with a weapon and backpack(40 pounds).The weight of the backpack gets progressively heavier, and the distance increases with every march.These marches take place take in unforgiving mountainous terrain.

Delta operators also go through a severe psychological testing.When the body and mind have reached its limits, they get tested on how they deal with interrogation and mental stress when they have already reached their physical limits.Not much is known about these tests, but they get tested to their psychological limits.Only the candidates with high levels of mental strength make it through testing.Delta has a 90% dropout rate.

The candidates that make it through the initial physical and psychological tests go on the intense 6-month Delta Operator Training Course.This course turns them into the ultimate soldiers.

### Training
According to the great book "Inside Delta Force" ,by Eric Haney, the Delta Force's Operator Training Course is estimated to last for 6 months.(Inside Delta Force,Eric Haney,2003) While the Operator Training Course(OTC) is continuously evolving, the following skills are always given focus:

### 1. Marksmanship
- The trainees are taught to shoot non-moving targets at point-blank without aiming.Afterwards, they then move on to mobile targets.
- Upon perfection of these shooting abilities, the trainees will move to clear rooms and shooting houses of enemy targets. Upon demonstration of sufficient abilities, hostages shall be mixed with the enemies.

### 2. Breaching and Demolition
- During this phase, the trainees will be taught to open various locks, including those on safes and cars.
- They will also be taught how to make a bomb and other explosives.

### 3. Combined skills

The FAA, FBI as well as other agencies are mobilized to provide assistance to this particular training option of OTC.The training includes training on commercial airliners.

## 4. Trade Craft

– in the initial phases of the OTC and the establishment of Delta Forces, CIA personnel were mobilized to train in this particular training portion

- In this phase, the trainees are taught various espionage techniques, such as those that involve surveillance monitoring, signals, pick-ups, brief encounters and dead drops.Delta Operators sometimes gets attached to the CIA to conduct missions.

5. Executive Protection – in the initial stages of the OTC and the establishment of the Delta Forces, the US Secret Service and US Department's Diplomatic Security Services provided consultation services for the Delta Force.

- Trainees undergo a driving course where they are taught how to utilize vehicles (whether just one or several) as offensive and defensive weapons.
- They are also taught strategies for diplomatic and VIP protection that were created by the DSS and the US Secret Service.

6.Other training includes the following: Advanced Parachuting, Advanced Climbing, Advanced Self- Defence and Scuba Diving.

## 7. Final Test

- This phase involves a final exam that forces the trainees to modify and utilize all the skills they have learned in their training.

## Joining Delta

The applicants that survive training and qualify to be a member of Delta get the title "Operator".Delta doesn't use ranks, and the members are referred to as Operators.

Delta Operators are unique in the US Army.They get a lot of freedom from the US Army to blend in with society as much as possible.They do not wear uniforms.When they do choose to wear a uniform in the field it's not US Army uniforms, they wear alternative uniforms with no marking or any forms of identification.They also have the freedom to grow beards and long hair.

## Missions and Clandestine Operations

The bulk of the Delta Force's operations is classified and may never be brought to the public's knowledge, although the details of some of their missions have been available in the public domain. There are numerous occasions that the Delta Forces have been placed on standby and operational plans developed, but the troop was stood down for many different reasons.

Following are some of the current and recent operations of the Delta Force:

- **2014 Raid in Northern Syria**

In an attempt to find kidnapped journalist James Foley as well as other American hostages, Delta Forces operators were inserted into northern Syria on 04 July 2014. Per information from witnesses, after tearing down anti-aircraft weapons, the Delta Forces operators attacked an ISIS base.

The ISIS base was torn down, and all ISIS soldiers were killed at the cost of an American, who sustained wounds during the operations. The operation was a failure since no hostages were found.

- **2014 Capture of Ahmed Abu Kahattala**

The Delta Force captured Ahmed Abu Kahattala on the weekend of 14 to 15 June 2014. The Delta Forces operators worked with contingent elite Intelligence Support Activity Operators who managed to track Ahmed Abu Khattala. The FBI agents made the arrest during this mission.

- **2013 Capture of Abuy Anas al-Lib**

On 05 October 2013, Abu Anas al-Liby was captured in Tripoli, Libya by the Delta Force who joined forces with operators from CIA's Special Activities Division, FBI agents and most probably, the Intelligence Support Activity Teams

- **2012 Benghazi Attack**

Two Delta Force operators, who were with 5 CIA operators, have escorted Glen Doherty during the Benghazi attack in 2012. This was to help the plagued Benghazi Embassy compound, after capturing a tiny aircraft in Tripoli. After ferocious fights, the rescue group and 2 Delta Force operators provided assistance in the evacuation of the surviving diplomatic personnel in the key Embassy in Tripoli.

Master Sargeant David R. Halbruner, an operator of the Delta force, has been given the award of "Distinguished Service Cross" for his courage and bravery. Another member, a marine connected to Delta force was also awarded with the "Navy Cross".

- ## 2009 Release of American Prisoner of War – Bowe Bergdahl

In a prisoner exchange that occurred on 31 May 2014, Bowe Bergdahl, an Army prisoner was handed over to the operators of the Delta Force. Bergdahl was captured by the Taliban group on 30 June 2009.

- ## 2005 Rescue of Roy Hallums, an American Hostage

The Delta Force operators rescued Roy Hallums on 07 September 2005. Hallums is an American contractor captured by an Iraqi group on 01 November 2004.

- ## 2004 Objective Medford

The Delta Force's A Squadron combined forces with the US Army's 160th SOAR and conducted a raid in an attempt to secure foreign workers at a compound close to Ramadi on 08 June 2004. The captors were caught off guard and immediately surrendered. The team's operation was a complete success.

# 11

# UNIT 1

## Special Air Service

The Special Air Service (SAS) is a unit of the British army established on 31 May 1950. The SAS is one of the main units that forms the UKSF or United Kingdom Special Forces.The SAS is the grandfather of all other Special Forces Units in the world.The SAS started the concept of small groups of highly trained men operating independently behind enemy lines.

The SAS, along with the Joint Special Forces Aviation Wing, 18 Signal Regiment of the UKSF, Special Forces Support Group or SFSG, Special Reconnaissance Regiment (SRR) and the Special Boat Service (SBS), all form the United Kingdom Special Forces (UKSF), under the authority of the Director of Special Forces.

## Location
The SAS base is located close to Hereford, England. They have been at this location since 1960.

## Brief History
The SAS was established during World War 2 . The SAS was the brainchild of David Stirling, who had an idea of a role for small, highly trained groups of men, operating behind enemy lines. In 1947, the SAS was reformed as an integral part of the Territorial Army and was called the 21st Battalion, SAS Regiment.

Later the SAS became part of the regular army regimental system and was renamed the 22 SAS Regiment(1952).The SAS operated all over the world in the shadows.They were an unknown weapon of the British government.They conducted successful campaigns all over the world without attracting attention.This anonymity ended in 1980 when the SAS was put under the spotlight with their successful raid of the Iranian Embassy in London.Suddenly the world sat up and took notice.Suddenly everyone had one question.Who is the SAS?

## Organization of the SAS

The British Special Air Service is composed of 4 squadrons.At any given time, there is about 55- 60 men is each squadron.Each squadron gets divided further into groups of 10-15.These small groups is called troops.Every troop has an officer in command, usually, a lieutenant or captain.

The SAS troops are put together with individuals with different skill sets.Every individual specializes in a form of military skill.Some of the skills are sniper, medic, signals, explosive expert, language expert and many other.

## Every Troop has a specialization:

- **Mobility Troop**– The Desert troop is probably the oldest troop in the SAS.They trace back their origin to the desert warfare of the second world war where they had many successful campaigns.The

Mobility Troop is known for using vehicles to reach their objectives. All members are trained in vehicle mechanics. The vehicles allow the SAS to mount heavy support weapons. They mount heavy machine guns, grenade launchers, and anti-tank missiles.

- **Boat Troop**– which are specially trained to conduct amphibious assignments. The SAS has the boat troop to conduct their own amphibious missions. They don't specialize in amphibious missions, but the boat troop gives them the capability for Insertion and extraction of patrols via small boats. They sometimes train with the Royal Navy's Special Boat Service. The members of boat troop are trained in scuba diving, kayaking and inflatable boats.
- **Air Troop** –The members of the Air Troop are masters of all types of parachuting. The majority of SAS members were members of the British Army's Elite Parachute Regiment. When they join the SAS Regiment, they take their airborne skills to the next level.
- **Mountain Troop** – The men of the mountain troop are trained to operate in extreme mountain conditions. They are specialists in cold weather survival, mountain climbing, and arctic warfare. They are skilled rock climbers and masters at Arctic survival techniques. In the mountains of Afganistan, the Mountain troop were used to hunt Taliban positions in the harsh mountain terrain.

### SAS Training and Selection

The SAS goes through one of the toughest selection processes in the world. The first part of the selection process takes place in the Brecon Beacons, Sennybridge, Wales. The Brecon Beacons is a harsh mountainous terrain in Wales. The dropout rate for the initial SAS selection in Wales is over 90%. To make it past this first phase is already a massive achievement.

### Selection

About 200 recruits start the phase one of the selection processes. The first thing recruits do at selection is to pass the Personal Fitness Test and the Annual Fitness Test. These are standard British Army fitness tests to get a basic assessment of recruits on arrival.

- **Mountain Phase**

This Mountain phase lasts approximately three weeks. After passing the initial tests, they start doing timed cross-country marches. Every day the marches get longer and the terrain more brutal. The loads that the soldiers carry get heavier every day. The marches reach its peak in a final march that is called "Endurance." "Endurance" is a 40-mile March that candidates must complete with a heavy backpack and weapon. They must complete this test in 20 hours. At the end of this test, they must run 4 miles in 30 minutes, and then swim 2 miles in 90 minutes. The Mountain phase has broken many hard men.

- **Jungle Phase**

The Candidates now go on a 4 week Jungle phase in Belize. Candidates receive training in navigation, patrolling and jungle survival. The extreme jungle conditions test recruits mental toughness. The conditions of the jungle test personal discipline to their limits.

- **Final Phase**

Soldiers who pass jungle training return to SAS headquarters in Hereford, England. At this stage of selection, the group will be very small, approximately 20% of the original 200. In this phase, they receive training in combat survival, foreign weapons, battle plans, and tactics. The final week has two parts; the first is the feared escape and evasion test. Candidates get placed in patrol groups and carry only a tin can filled with survival equipment. Then they got navigation instructions and told to start marching. In the test, candidates get hunted down by infantry units.

This test is arguably the hardest and will test the mental toughness of every candidate past their known limits. The possibility of special forces soldiers to be taken prisoner behind enemy lines is high, so these tests are taken extremely seriously.

Eventually, candidates get caught by the "enemy" patrol and gets interrogated. Candidates are treated in extremely bad ways by instructors, and they must resist extreme physical and mental discomfort. Candidates at this stage will be extremely sleep deprived, dehydrated and will be put in physically stressful positions while being questioned.

Approximately 10-15% of the original 200 will make it through selection. The candidates who make it trough the final phase of training receives the famous SAS Wings. The new SAS operators will be probationary members and will receive continuation training.

Having passed the taxing process of selection and earned their SAS wings, SAS recruits will enter a training phase that in some aspects, never stops. SAS soldiers continuously learn new abilities and refine those that they already have.

### The following are some details on the SAS roles and training processes:
### · Gathering Intelligence

The SAS train in a wide range of intelligence gathering methods. This basically comes down to slipping in behind enemy lines and gathering information. Training includes extracting after the mission is done. This work is of vital importance before conventional forces enter into an area.

### · Precision Attacks Behind Enemy Lines

The SAS has been disrupting enemy activity all over the world for a long time. The SAS train in various methods of disrupting enemy movement, communications and supply lines.

### · Helping and Training Foreign Forces

The SAS members get trained in skills to help and train foreign militaries.These skills include negotiation, language training , advanced medical training and foreign weapon training.

• **Security Training**

The SAS are trained in the close protection of senior military officers, politicians and other important individuals.This type training is an ongoing process in the regiment.

• **Counter-Terrorism Training**

One squadron shall be assigned to do counter-terrorism assignments. After obtaining the proper speed with the counter-terrorism techniques, the engage squadron divides into two sections. One squadron engages in exercises and is on a 24-hour warning to respond; the other squadron performs training activities at the different SAS training institutions and gets placed on standby for any possible situation.

• **Government Agencies**

SAS operators sometimes get attached to agencies like the MI5 and MI6.They fit into this role easily due to their highly adaptable training.

**The Killing House**

The SAS Troops perform the majority of their counter-terrorism training in a uniquely constructed house located at the SAS Headquarters, referred to as the "Killing House". This special facility is used to develop the SAS soldier's Close Quarter Battle (CQB) abilities. The CQG strategies are practiced over and over until the different maneuvers a reflex action for the operators.

**- Building Attacks**

When they have to practice getting into buildings, the SAS troops will utilize uniquely established structures. This training phase specifically includes the following:

- Blowing access holes into the building's sides with the use of explosives
- Obtaining access through the ladders – either attached to the roofs of Range Rovers or carried on foot
- Abseiling down the building sides from the roof or into the rooftops from a helicopter

### –Tubular Assaults

Terrorist groups around the world are known to take hostages aboard coaches, busses and trains. The SAS troops constantly train in attacking such targets. The SAS training facilities include a railway tracks along with railway carriages where the SAS troops practice attacking hijacked trains and airplanes.

### The following are some of the current and recent

## operations of the SAS:

- 2009 – 22 SAS turns its attention to Afghanistan
- 2003 – SAS troops go in ahead of the major allied attack of Iraq. During the post-attack in Iraq, troupes from 22 SAS rotate through troops of Task Force Black, a unique forces task team established to attack insurgents.
- 2001 – SAS attack Taliban and Al Qaeda in Afghanistan
- 2000 – The SAS, along with British Paratroopers (Parachute Regiment) and the SBS, free British military men from the Sierra Leone rebels in a brave rescue assignment.
- 1991 – The SAS set foot and patrolled deep behind the Iraqi lines on operations to take down Saddam Hussein's scud launchers
- 1988 – The SAS undercover troupes shoots and kills and IRA active force unit in Gibraltar

# 12

# Conclusion

I want to thank you for reading this book! I sincerely hope that you received value from it!

If you received value from this book, I want to ask you for a favour. Would you be kind enough to leave a review for this book on Amazon?

any usage or abuse of any policies, processes, or directions contained within is the solitary and utter responsibility of the recipient reader. Under no circumstances will any legal responsibility or blame be held against the publisher for any reparation, damages, or monetary loss due to the information herein, either directly or indirectly.

Respective authors own all copyrights not held by the publisher.

The information herein is offered for informational purposes solely, and is universal as so. The presentation of the information is without contract or any type of guarantee assurance.

The trademarks that are used are without any consent, and the publication of the trademark is without permission or backing by the trademark owner. All trademarks and brands within this book are for clarifying purposes only and are the owned by the owners themselves, not affiliated with this document.

CPSIA information can be obtained
at www.ICGtesting.com
Printed in the USA
LVHW021607240121
677358LV00013B/1857